# Manifest an Epic Year In 100 Days

By: Modjossorica Elysee

Manifest an Epic Year In 100 Days by **Modjossorica Elysee**
P.O. Box 121136 Boston, MA 02112
www.ricaelysee.com
© 2021 Modjossorica Elysee

ISBN: 9798713470708

This workbook is dedicated to all the women who made me stronger, smarter, and bold.

# This Workbook Belongs to

_______________________________

# How to Use this Workbook

One of the most important lessons I learned when building my career in business has been that it is a journey of self-discovery. You will learn that you enjoy and dislike parts of the process but it makes you stronger.

Another lesson for me during my journey in entrepreneurship was the power of manifestation. It was so key for me to want and focus the success I wanted to have. We manifest every day the things we want. Yet the way to get what we want has to do with the power and energy individual puts towards it. If you are scared or fearful then it will manifest itself into failure.

Yet if you intensely focus on these hopes, dreams and plans in a positive manner it will make them reality.

This workbook is designed to get you to focus on the questions that will give you clarity building the life and business that you want. Using energy and belief to create your reality with this workbook.

Here are a few tips for success with this workbook:

1.  Every day for the next 100 days answer <u>ONE</u> Manifestation prompt question.

2.  Make sure to answer the questions completely and honestly.

3.  Ask the Universe for the ability to learn, build and execute while you review your answers.

4.  Trust the process and manifest the success you desire.

5.  Finally clear the resistance in your path with these answer

# Manifest the Life & Business You Deserve

# MANIFESTATION QUESTION OF THE DAY:

What are 10 obvious things that make me happy?

## MANIFESTATION QUESTION OF THE DAY:

What are 10 things that I don't appreciate as much as I should?

## MANIFESTATION QUESTION OF THE DAY:

What activities bring me the most joy? What could I do more of to increase my happiness?

## MANIFESTATION QUESTION OF THE DAY:

What qualities do I love about myself?

## MANIFESTATION QUESTION OF THE DAY:

What qualities do I admire in other people/my hero? How can I cultivate those qualities in myself?

## MANIFESTATION QUESTION OF THE DAY:

How often do I feel stressed out or anxious? What triggers those feelings? Can I create a system that helps me cope with those feelings?

## MANIFESTATION QUESTION OF THE DAY:

When I close my eyes and picture my dream life, what do I see or feel? What small daily actions can get me from here to there?

## MANIFESTATION QUESTION OF THE DAY:

Do the accounts I follow on social media make me feel good or bad about myself? What do I need to see more of and less of to care for my mental health?

## MANIFESTATION QUESTION OF THE DAY:

What limiting beliefs do I need to change so I can move towards my goals?

## MANIFESTATION QUESTION OF THE DAY:

What habits could I change to improve my life?

## MANIFESTATION QUESTION OF THE DAY:

What does success look like to me? If I was always successful what would that look like?

## MANIFESTATION QUESTION OF THE DAY:

What does failure look like to me? If I don't succeed at something the first time is it fair to call that failure?

## MANIFESTATION QUESTION OF THE DAY:

What do I fear most? If I wasn't afraid what would I do?

## MANIFESTATION QUESTION OF THE DAY:

Is my lifestyle as healthy as it could be? What are a few simple ways I could improve?

MANIFESTATION QUESTION OF THE DAY:

## MANIFESTATION QUESTION OF THE DAY:

What are some of my accomplishments, big and small?

## MANIFESTATION QUESTION OF THE DAY:

Do I believe I'm worthy of my dreams and goals? If not how will I work to change that?

## MANIFESTATION QUESTION OF THE DAY:

What does a perfect day in my life look like? How can I gradually shift my routines to make that a daily reality?

## MANIFESTATION QUESTION OF THE DAY:

What people or situations drain my energy? What strategy can I create to deal with or avoid those situations?

## MANIFESTATION QUESTION OF THE DAY:

What would make me happy right now?

## MANIFESTATION QUESTION OF THE DAY:

What's draining my energy?

# MANIFESTATION QUESTION OF THE DAY:

What do I want to learn more about?

## MANIFESTATION QUESTION OF THE DAY:

Who are 3 people I admire? Why?

## MANIFESTATION QUESTION OF THE DAY:

How can I be more like those I admire?

## MANIFESTATION QUESTION OF THE DAY:

How am I already demonstrating traits I admire?

## MANIFESTATION QUESTION OF THE DAY:

How do I define success?

## MANIFESTATION QUESTION OF THE DAY:

What does self-care look like for me?

## MANIFESTATION QUESTION OF THE DAY:

What accomplishments am I proud of from last month?

## MANIFESTATION QUESTION OF THE DAY:

What is a short term goal I am certain I can achieve?

# MANIFESTATION QUESTION OF THE DAY:

What does my ideal day look like? (ie. where are you? who are you with, and what are you doing?)

## MANIFESTATION QUESTION OF THE DAY:

What can I de-clutter physically or emotionally to find more ease and simplicity?

## MANIFESTATION QUESTION OF THE DAY:

How do I feel today, really? Why?

## MANIFESTATION QUESTION OF THE DAY:

What's something that's been a lot on my mind lately? What can I do about it?

## MANIFESTATION QUESTION OF THE DAY:

What's my most recurrent feeling?

## MANIFESTATION QUESTION OF THE DAY:

How do I feel about my daily routine? Do I like what I do day after day? Why?

## MANIFESTATION QUESTION OF THE DAY:

What do I think about my daily habits?

## MANIFESTATION QUESTION OF THE DAY:

What do I dislike the most about my life?

## MANIFESTATION QUESTION OF THE DAY:

What do I need more of in my life? Why?

## MANIFESTATION QUESTION OF THE DAY:

What do I need less of in my life? Why?

## Manifestation Question of the Day:

What do I love the most about myself and my life? Name at least three things.

___________________________________________

___________________________________________

## MANIFESTATION QUESTION OF THE DAY:

How much has my life changed in the past year? How do I feel about that?

___________________________________________

___________________________________________

___________________________________________

___________________________________________

___________________________________________

___________________________________________

___________________________________________

___________________________________________

___________________________________________

___________________________________________

___________________________________________

___________________________________________

___________________________________________

___________________________________________

___________________________________________

___________________________________________

___________________________________________

___________________________________________

___________________________________________

___________________________________________

## MANIFESTATION QUESTION OF THE DAY:

Name at least three things that make you feel proud?

## MANIFESTATION QUESTION OF THE DAY:

What do I need to let go of? (People, resentment, bitterness, memories)

_______________________________________________

_______________________________________________

## MANIFESTATION QUESTION OF THE DAY:

Name the three most important life lessons you've learned so far.

_______________________________________________

_______________________________________________

_______________________________________________

_______________________________________________

_______________________________________________

_______________________________________________

_______________________________________________

_______________________________________________

_______________________________________________

_______________________________________________

_______________________________________________

_______________________________________________

_______________________________________________

_______________________________________________

_______________________________________________

_______________________________________________

_______________________________________________

_______________________________________________

_______________________________________________

_______________________________________________

_______________________________________________

_______________________________________________

## MANIFESTATION QUESTION OF THE DAY:

When have I felt the most motivated?

_______________________________________________

_______________________________________________

_______________________________________________

_______________________________________________

_______________________________________________

_______________________________________________

_______________________________________________

_______________________________________________

_______________________________________________

_______________________________________________

_______________________________________________

_______________________________________________

_______________________________________________

_______________________________________________

_______________________________________________

_______________________________________________

_______________________________________________

_______________________________________________

## MANIFESTATION QUESTION OF THE DAY:

## MANIFESTATION QUESTION OF THE DAY:

What's preventing me from pursuing the things I want to pursue?

MANIFESTATION QUESTION OF THE DAY:

## MANIFESTATION QUESTION OF THE DAY:

What am I willing to sacrifice now to have my dream life later?

# MANIFESTATION QUESTION OF THE DAY:

What bothers me?

## MANIFESTATION QUESTION OF THE DAY:

Which personality trait in others makes me like them immediately? What does that say about me?

## MANIFESTATION QUESTION OF THE DAY:

What's the most important thing to me when it comes to relationships?

## MANIFESTATION QUESTION OF THE DAY:

What makes me feel useful and that I'm helping others?

## MANIFESTATION QUESTION OF THE DAY:

Identify your negative self-talk. What are the doubts I plant in my own mind?

## MANIFESTATION QUESTION OF THE DAY:

Which positive statements could I use to replace my negative self-talk?

## MANIFESTATION QUESTION OF THE DAY:

What positive things could others say about me? Do I believe they're true? Why?

_________________________________________________

_________________________________________________

## MANIFESTATION QUESTION OF THE DAY:

What negative things could others say about me? Do I believe they're true? Why?

_________________________________________________

_________________________________________________

_________________________________________________

_________________________________________________

_________________________________________________

_________________________________________________

_________________________________________________

_________________________________________________

_________________________________________________

_________________________________________________

_________________________________________________

_________________________________________________

_________________________________________________

_________________________________________________

_________________________________________________

_________________________________________________

_________________________________________________

_________________________________________________

_________________________________________________

MANIFESTATION QUESTION OF THE DAY:

## MANIFESTATION QUESTION OF THE DAY:

If I keep doing the same things I'm doing right now, will I have my dream life in two or three years? If not, will I at least be closer?

_______________________________________________

_______________________________________________

## MANIFESTATION QUESTION OF THE DAY:

How do I want to feel on a daily basis? Inspired, engaged, motivated, accomplished, relaxed?

_______________________________________________

_______________________________________________

_______________________________________________

_______________________________________________

_______________________________________________

_______________________________________________

_______________________________________________

_______________________________________________

_______________________________________________

_______________________________________________

_______________________________________________

_______________________________________________

_______________________________________________

_______________________________________________

_______________________________________________

_______________________________________________

_______________________________________________

_______________________________________________

_______________________________________________

_________________________________________________

# MANIFESTATION QUESTION OF THE DAY:

What do I see in others or other's life that I want for me? Why?

_________________________________________________

_________________________________________________

_________________________________________________

_________________________________________________

_________________________________________________

_________________________________________________

_________________________________________________

_________________________________________________

_________________________________________________

_________________________________________________

_________________________________________________

_________________________________________________

_________________________________________________

_________________________________________________

_________________________________________________

_________________________________________________

_________________________________________________

MANIFESTATION QUESTION OF THE DAY:

## MANIFESTATION QUESTION OF THE DAY:

What's the most important thing to me right now?

---

## MANIFESTATION QUESTION OF THE DAY:

How do I feel today, really? Why? How different is this feeling from the feeling I described on day #1?

## MANIFESTATION QUESTION OF THE DAY:

If the energy of your past year could be encapsulated by one word, what would that word be?

## MANIFESTATION QUESTION OF THE DAY:

What were your big wins this year?

## MANIFESTATION QUESTION OF THE DAY:

What were your small wins this year?

## MANIFESTATION QUESTION OF THE DAY:

What were your challenges this year?

## MANIFESTATION QUESTION OF THE DAY:

For every challenge on your list, write down 1 (or more) lessons, tools, or gifts your challenges gave you this year?

## MANIFESTATION QUESTION OF THE DAY:

What do you need to shed or leave behind from this past year?

## MANIFESTATION QUESTION OF THE DAY:

Who were the most integral people in your life this past year?

## MANIFESTATION QUESTION OF THE DAY:

How did these people support you, teach you or help you to grow?

_______________________________________________

_______________________________________________

## MANIFESTATION QUESTION OF THE DAY:

Regarding physical health, what health, wellness and fitness practices were most beneficial and enjoyable for you this year?

_______________________________________________

_______________________________________________

_______________________________________________

_______________________________________________

_______________________________________________

_______________________________________________

_______________________________________________

_______________________________________________

_______________________________________________

_______________________________________________

_______________________________________________

_______________________________________________

_______________________________________________

_______________________________________________

_______________________________________________

_______________________________________________

_______________________________________________

_______________________________________________

_______________________________________________

_______________________________________________

## MANIFESTATION QUESTION OF THE DAY:

What health, wellness and fitness practices were the most challenging or perhaps detrimental?

## MANIFESTATION QUESTION OF THE DAY:

With your health last year in mind, what are your health goals for this coming year?

_______________________________________________

_______________________________________________

## MANIFESTATION QUESTION OF THE DAY:

Regarding financial health, what practices (if any) did you implement in the past year that were of benefit?

_______________________________________________

_______________________________________________

_______________________________________________

_______________________________________________

_______________________________________________

_______________________________________________

_______________________________________________

_______________________________________________

_______________________________________________

_______________________________________________

_______________________________________________

_______________________________________________

_______________________________________________

_______________________________________________

_______________________________________________

_______________________________________________

_______________________________________________

_______________________________________________

## MANIFESTATION QUESTION OF THE DAY:

What financial practices will you start (or continue) in the coming year to grow wealth and become financially stable?

## MANIFESTATION QUESTION OF THE DAY:

What are your overall finance goals for this coming year?

---

## MANIFESTATION QUESTION OF THE DAY:

What are your career or vocation goals for this coming year?

## MANIFESTATION QUESTION OF THE DAY:

What are your personal goals or intentions for this coming year?

_______________________________________________

_______________________________________________

## MANIFESTATION QUESTION OF THE DAY:

Keeping these goals in mind, what is one over-arching intention you would like to set for this coming year?

_______________________________________________

_______________________________________________

_______________________________________________

_______________________________________________

_______________________________________________

_______________________________________________

_______________________________________________

_______________________________________________

_______________________________________________

_______________________________________________

_______________________________________________

_______________________________________________

_______________________________________________

_______________________________________________

_______________________________________________

_______________________________________________

_______________________________________________

_______________________________________________

_______________________________________________

_______________________________________________

## MANIFESTATION QUESTION OF THE DAY:

What is one small thing you are manifesting for this coming year?

## MANIFESTATION QUESTION OF THE DAY:

What is one big thing you are manifesting for this coming year?

# MANIFESTATION QUESTION OF THE DAY:

What are 4 ways you will push yourself out of your comfort zone this year?

# MANIFESTATION QUESTION OF THE DAY:

At the end of this coming year what is the ONE thing you want to have accomplished or maintained commitment to?

## MANIFESTATION QUESTION OF THE DAY:

Brainstorm 10-20 words that encapsulate the energy that you're calling in to your commitment year. Reflect and then choose ONE WORD that reflects the overall intention you'd like to set for this coming year. This is your "word of the year."

_______________________________________________

_______________________________________________

## MANIFESTATION QUESTION OF THE DAY:

What's something that's been on my mind lately?

_______________________________________________

_______________________________________________

_______________________________________________

_______________________________________________

_______________________________________________

_______________________________________________

_______________________________________________

_______________________________________________

_______________________________________________

_______________________________________________

_______________________________________________

_______________________________________________

_______________________________________________

_______________________________________________

_______________________________________________

_______________________________________________

_______________________________________________

_______________________________________________

_______________________________________________

_______________________________________________

## MANIFESTATION QUESTION OF THE DAY:

What do I think about my daily habits?

## MANIFESTATION QUESTION OF THE DAY:

What am I willing to sacrifice to have my dream life?

## MANIFESTATION QUESTION OF THE DAY:

What makes me like people immediately?

## MANIFESTATION QUESTION OF THE DAY:

What do I dislike the most about my life?

MANIFESTATION QUESTION OF THE DAY:

## MANIFESTATION QUESTION OF THE DAY:

Name at least three things that make you feel proud?

---

## MANIFESTATION QUESTION OF THE DAY:

What's the most important thing to me right now?

## MANIFESTATION QUESTION OF THE DAY:

What's my most recurrent feeling?

_______________________________________________

_______________________________________________

## MANIFESTATION QUESTION OF THE DAY:

How do I want to feel on a daily basis?

_______________________________________________

_______________________________________________

_______________________________________________

_______________________________________________

_______________________________________________

_______________________________________________

_______________________________________________

_______________________________________________

_______________________________________________

_______________________________________________

_______________________________________________

_______________________________________________

_______________________________________________

_______________________________________________

_______________________________________________

_______________________________________________

_______________________________________________

_______________________________________________

_______________________________________________

_______________________________________________

## MANIFESTATION QUESTION OF THE DAY:

What's preventing me from pursuing my dreams?

______________________________________________

______________________________________________

## MANIFESTATION QUESTION OF THE DAY:

What makes me feel useful and that I'm helping others?

______________________________________________

______________________________________________

______________________________________________

______________________________________________

______________________________________________

______________________________________________

______________________________________________

______________________________________________

______________________________________________

______________________________________________

______________________________________________

______________________________________________

______________________________________________

______________________________________________

______________________________________________

______________________________________________

______________________________________________

______________________________________________

______________________________________________

## MANIFESTATION QUESTION OF THE DAY:

## MANIFESTATION QUESTION OF THE DAY:

How do I feel today, really? Why?

---

---

## MANIFESTATION QUESTION OF THE DAY:

When have I felt the most motivated?

_______________________________________________

## MANIFESTATION QUESTION OF THE DAY:

What do I like the most about my life?

_______________________________________________
_______________________________________________
_______________________________________________
_______________________________________________
_______________________________________________
_______________________________________________
_______________________________________________
_______________________________________________
_______________________________________________
_______________________________________________
_______________________________________________
_______________________________________________
_______________________________________________
_______________________________________________
_______________________________________________
_______________________________________________
_______________________________________________
_______________________________________________
_______________________________________________

## MANIFESTATION QUESTION OF THE DAY:

What do I need to let go of?

## MANIFESTATION QUESTION OF THE DAY:

Which positive things could I say about myself?

## MANIFESTATION QUESTION OF THE DAY:

What bothers me?

MANIFESTATION QUESTION OF THE DAY:

## MANIFESTATION QUESTION OF THE DAY:

What do I see in others or other's life that I want for me?

_______________________________

_______________________________

## MANIFESTATION QUESTION OF THE DAY:

What do I value in relationships?

_______________________________

_______________________________

_______________________________

_______________________________

_______________________________

_______________________________

_______________________________

_______________________________

_______________________________

_______________________________

_______________________________

_______________________________

_______________________________

_______________________________

_______________________________

_______________________________

_______________________________

_______________________________

_______________________________

_______________________________

MANIFESTATION QUESTION OF THE DAY:

_______________________________________________

_______________________________________________

## GOOD BYE LOVE NOTE

Congratulations on reaching the end of this workbook!  I know what was involved in getting through these pages. I am excited that you are accomplishing the first step in building your journey as an entrepreneur. Kicking butt with this workbook in record breaking time and in not only meeting your goal but surpassing it! I'm so proud of you for setting your sights high and making every effort to achieve that goal. You truly are leading by example to ensure your continuing reputation for excellence. You worked hard and proved to yourself and everyone what you are capable of. Best wishes for continued success.

# HI THERE I'M RICA!

I am a funded Black Women entrepreneur in tech. I have been a successful community organizer, marketer, and fundraising executive. I have founded multiple companies focused on building up women. I have used my lessons in building my companies to build multiple workbooks to give entrepreneurs the pointers I wish I knew before I got started. This manifestation workbook is personal dive into self-discovery to help you build not only the business you want but the life you want with deeper understanding of yourself.

If you want to connect with me make sure to use hashtag #businessbytes or connecting with me on social media @ricatheceo on IG.